Contents

Lairy hair

So a trip to the hairdressers is bliss, right? A cut every six weeks to keep the cool look? Or is your fantasy that one day you might be hairdresser to pop and film stars? Snipping away at Posh's locks and brushing Beckham's barnet! Well, think some more, as hair has a flair for being a bit, you might say ... lairy, and it does not always play fair.

Get this – you think you are a hairdresser "extraordinaire". There is a customer in the salon chair. They show you a pop star in a mag and say they need to look as good as that.

You wash the hair.
You trim the hair.
It does not look good.

You snip a bit more ... and more ... and more. The customer's hair does not match the pop star's hair yet. The air is full of hair and you are full of despair.

Oops!

Problem is you have gone too far – ever had a go at repairing hair? Will hair do what you want? No way! Hair will not play fair! You end up giving the customer their money back. Well, you can't give the hair back, can you?

And what happens when you get asked to do a mad hair cut? You can't hoot and snort when a lad pops in and asks for a cut that looks as if it was in fashion when your grandad was a kid!

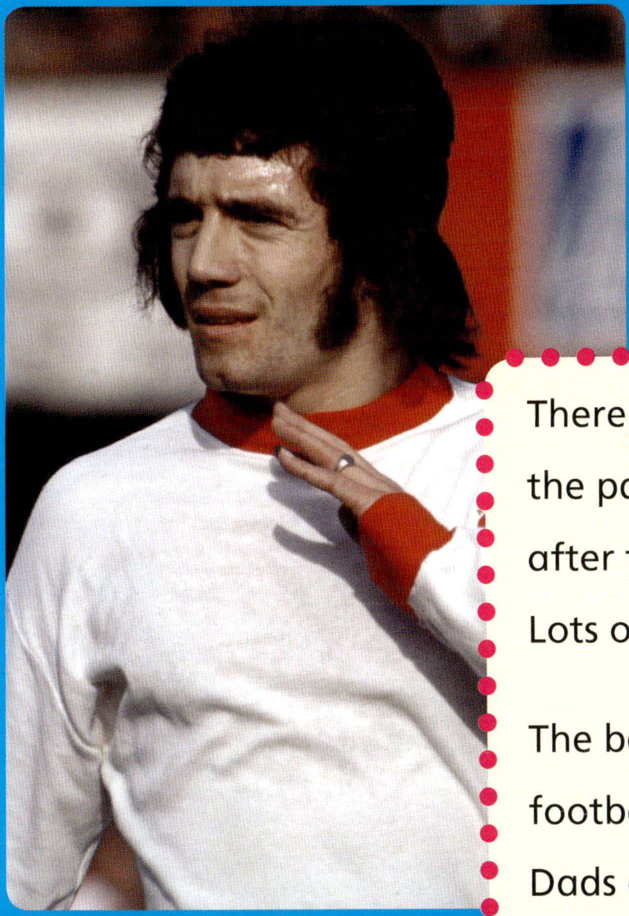

There have been some bizarre haircuts in the past – one was called a mullet after the tailfin of a mullet fish! Lots of football stars had this cut.

The best known "mullet man" was a football star of the 70s, Kevin Keegan. Dads and lads rushed to off to get the cool Keegan look.

Hair is so odd. Still want to spend days on end playing with hair?

Lairy hair facts

Lairy hair fact number 1

Hair is the fastest – growing tissue on your body! Okay, you might say, that's not so odd. Try this then ...

Lairy hair fact number 2

A loss of 100 hairs a day is normal!

Still not impressed? Here is lairy hair fact number 3

A hair could hold the weight of a 100gram choccy bar before snapping. Did you say boring? That's it then – you get the lairiest hair fact of all. This will shock you (get a chair).

Lairy hair fact number 4

An insect called a wood roach scoffs as much hair as it can.

Yuck! Yes, it's a fact. Hair has a chemical called keratin in it and that keep the insect's shell strong!

But don't let me put you off. A hairdresser to the top stars can get as much as £600 for giving them a haircut! Now where did I put that hairbrush ...

What sort of football fan are you - fanatical, fair or a flop?

Think you know? Check first in this fun football quiz!

1) A red card is

a) given when you have not played well.

b) shown when you will be sent off the pitch for being a dirty player.

c) what you get from a craft shop.

2) A penalty shoot out is

a) When teams keep playing until there is a winner.

b) When the scores are a draw and you need a winner, so players keep shooting at the net. First to score the most is the winner.

c) sounds a bit odd – is it to do with a gun going off?

3) The penalty spot is

a) a circle on the pitch that you stand on for a penalty kick.

b) the spot the ball is put on for a penalty kick.

c) what you get on the end of your nose in your teens.

4) If you hit the post, you

a) whirl and twirl in circles and then crash into the goal post.

b) try to score but the ball hits the goal post first.

c) do a very nasty thing to that girl who delivers letters.

5) The World Cup is

a) a cup for thirsty players to drink from.

b) what every footballer in the world is stirred up to win.

c) good to put daffodils in to brighten up the locker rooms.

6) Studs are

a) to do with boots but I don't know what they are for.

b) on the bottom of boots to give players a firm grip on a slippy pitch.

c) I know this one – they are little gold things you put in your ears.

The referee has blown the whistle.

Tot up your scores. If you got:

Mostly As

You know a bit of football stuff but you are still hitting the post, 3–0.

You are a fair football fan.

Mostly Bs

Right in the back of the net. Top score 6–0.

You are a fanatical football fan.

Mostly Cs

I will try not to smirk. Do you know what a football is?

You didn't get to kick-off, 0-0.

You are a flop of a football fan.

Norman Knight, time-travelling superstar

Ashton Villa have got to their first FA Cup semi, one step away from Wembley, and are playing West Hum. But time is running out. Only one man can save them: Norman Knight, a player picked up from Stockport County (in 1895).

... and as we go into the last moments of this epic FA Cup semi it looks as if Ashton Villa are about to go out. One-nil down, and with star player Rich Bird flat out on the ground after a bad foul. What do you think Ray? Is Villa's proud cup run about to end?

It looks that way, Des.

But hang on, is that time-travelling superstar Norman Knight I see about to come on the pitch, Ray?
Des
Yes, I think so, Des.
Ray
He's putting his book down (after putting his book mark in), finishing his beef sandwich and stepping out onto the pitch. What an odd sight he is, with his slick hair, black tash, long shorts, wooden shinpads and army boots.
.com
Very odd, Des.
Dickens

He's got the ball now and is dribbling rings round the defence. He shoots ... the ball hits Lumplard's hand ... penalty! And Lumplard is sent off!

Norman Knight has won a penalty in the last seconds of the match. But what's going on? Norman's angry. He's telling the ref off! "Nonsense!" he's saying, "it's not a penalty! That's unfair!" But the ref is in no doubt. It is a penalty, and Knight will take it himself. Astonishing! What do you think, Ray?

It's astonishing, Des.

But what's Norman doing? He seems to be saying sorry to the goalie. He's patting him on the back and wishing him luck. Now he's looking away from the goal. He's shooting at the corner flag! Astounding! Norman Knight has kicked the ball at the corner flag. Ray?

Astounding, Des.

There isn't a sound round the ground. Sixty thousand fans are stunned. But the match has started again, and with just seconds to go Villa are on the attack. The ball is bouncing about by the West Hum goal. Knight pounces and sends it crashing into the back of the net. That's it! It's the end of the game! The West Hum men are on their knees. The Villa lads are jumping on Knight, men are trying to hug him and kiss him, but he's pushing them off. What's he saying, Ray?

He's telling them to be men, not silly infants, Des. He's telling them to show respect for the West Hum lads and help them off the ground.

Astonishing. He's asking them to say thanks to the ref! And now the Villa fans are chanting. "One Norman Knight! There's only one Norman Knight!" they are singing.

They are right there, Des!

Troy Tomato cooks up a storm

Would you employ this man as a chef? He can hardly boil an egg!

In the TV kitchen

Today, Joy Floyd meets the well-known chef Troy Tomato, and chats to him as he cooks.

Joy: Good morning!
In today's show,
Troy is going to show us how to cook some of his top dishes.

Join us in the TV kitchen!

You've been cooking since you were a boy, haven't you, Troy?

Troy: Yes - my Uncle Roy had some good tips, and my Auntie Septic always told me to wash my hands first.
You won't be disappointed today, Joy. I think you'll enjoy my food.

Joy: What's your best dish?

Troy: I do a corking hot dog and chips.
And my boil-in-the-bag fish isn't bad.
But it's not all about posh nosh.
Let me show you.

Joy: Oh yes, that sounds delightful!

Troy: First, I'm going to cook bangers and mash, and pancakes.

Peel the spuds – ouch, try not to peel your fingers – and boil them in a pan (the spuds, not your fingers).

Put some foil on top of the bangers, and put them in the oven.

Troy: As they're cooking, I'll start the pancakes. Stir up your batter – do you want a spoonful?

Joy: Er, no, thanks. It looks a bit lumpy.

Troy: Then swirl the oil in a non-stick pan.
When it's hot, tip in some batter
– and let it cook.

Then – toss!

Joy: The pancake's stuck to the roof, Troy.

Troy: That's okay – I'll just cook some more …

Joy: What was that noise – oh, no, it's the oven! You left the bangers in for too long, and it's blown up!

Troy: Oops! They were bangers all right. Next, mash the spuds – and squirt lots of ketchup on the top …

Joy: Look at my dress, Troy! I'm getting a bit annoyed!

Troy: So–ree! Well, the bangers are spoiled.

Joy: So is my best silk dress!

Troy: Let's try a boiled egg. I can't spoil a boiled egg, can I? Boil your water for about three mins – it's not boiling yet so I'll do a crab salad. Pick up your crab, like so – ouch! My finger! I forgot – first, kill your crab!

Joy: What's that hissing noise, Troy?

Troy: It's the water! Slight hitch – it's all boiled away – and I forgot to put the egg in! No boiled egg, then. Next, I'm going to cook a joint of beef – sirloin is good – with garlic and chilli. Mix up some garlic and chilli, and test it by putting a bit in your mouth – ouch! Aaargh! I forgot – chilli is hot!

Troy: Rub the garlic and chilli into the joint.
Tip some oil into a pan, and add the joint. Cook it on the ring until it's golden, and then put it in the oven – Oh, no, I forgot. I've blown the oven up, haven't I? Well …

Joy: Troy, you've put too much oil in the pan! It's on fire! Quick! Put it out! Don't just flap a cloth at it!
Stop the cameras …

Don't just flap a cloth at it!
You've destroyed the set, you moron!

Our fantastic TV kitchen is a mess!

Troy: I'm sorry, Joy. I think I'll just stick to cooking hot dog and chips. Well, let's forget the chips.

Joy: And the hot dog!

Troy: Oh, I almost forgot.
Can I sell you my cookbook?
It's called "Troy Tomato Cooks Up a Storm".
It's chock full of top tips, and it's just £75.99 …

Joy: Grrr … oh, what's the point?

I quit!

Room rage!

Can't find your black T-shirt?

Can't face going into your room?

Is it in a bit of a state?

Does your mum go ape about it, and say, "Who chucked the hand grenade?"

Are you a victim of ... **room rage?**

All teenage kids are the same – male and female!

But you can make your room a cool place to chill out with your mates. Don't blame your mum – it's your job!

It's never too late to change your ways.

get it sorted!

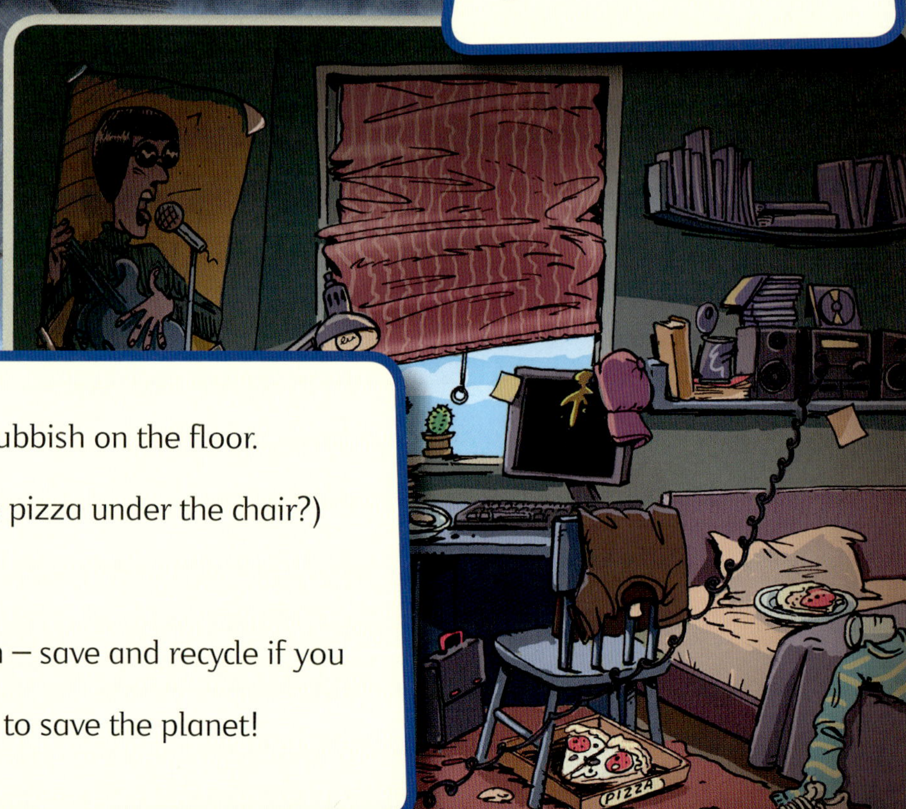

1) First, pick up all the rubbish on the floor.

(Is that a bit of Sunday's pizza under the chair?)

Throw it into a binbag.

Don't forget to be green – save and recycle if you can. It's not cheesy – it's to save the planet!

2) Take out all the dirty mugs and plates. Yes, and check under the bed. Bin that bit of stale cake left over from your last birthday party!

3) Pick up all the dirty socks and put them in the washing basket. Put a peg on your nose if you need to!

4) Hang up your shirts and your trackie bottoms. T-shirts, pants and socks go on a shelf, not on the floor, or the chair, or the lampshade!

5) Collect all the footie boots, laces, skates and put them in a corner. Important: skates left on stairs are a no-no.

6) Vacuum the carpet – it's that noisy electric thing that sucks up dirt! Your mum will be v impressed!

7) Shake out your sheets and pillow cases, and make the bed. It will feel good when you wake up in the morning. (Get rid of all the pet hairs and fluff. Don't let your Great Dane sleep on the bed – or your ten long-haired cats!)

8) Put your books in the bookcase or on the shelf. But first, replace any loose pages, and fix them with sticky tape. If it's a good story, it helps if you can see the ending!

9) School books, pens, felt tips, crayons, pencils (in pencil case!) go on your desk or table! Ditto your MP3 player, laptop or games.

10) You may have toys, model planes, space-ships, games etc that you have grown out of. Put them in a bag, so you can take them to a car boot sale. You may make lots of cash!

11) Look in your school bag. Chuck out all the apple cores, stale sandwiches that are well past their sell-by date, sweet wrappers and crisp packets.

12) Put your hairbrush, hair gel, stuff for spots, etc. in the bathroom. But watch out for your big brother – he may try to nick them when you're not looking!

13) Think about the walls. If your posters are flapping about, fix them with sticky-tack. Maybe you can get some fresh ones with cars on, or sports, or pop stars and bands. Ask if you can have a cork pinboard, so you can pin up photos, postcards, art and other cool stuff.

14) Last of all, put your name on the door:

"Jake's room – knock before you come in!"

(You should make your family knock so you can prepare them for the shock of seeing your room so tidy!)

Now you can enjoy your cool bedroom!

But don't forget – no more stale sandwiches, and stinky socks, and sticky bits of fluff. Give your room a make-over every week, and then you can have your mates round and you can get it all messy again!

Lairy Hair (air)

Green words: *Say the sounds. Say the word.*

hair air flair chair fair lairy extraordinaire

Say the syllables. Say the word.

des'pair → despair rep'air → repair

Say the root word. Say the whole word.

repair → repairing

Red words:

to your you some does are their they there what where call all could of was want go* so* be*

Challenge words:

customer money fashion can't wash bizarre lairiest tailfin football number tissue try weight hold roach chemical keratin now

Vocabulary check:

lairy *flashy or behaving outrageously*

extraordinaire *excellent or outstanding*

bizarre *very strange and weird*

barnet *slang word for hair*

What sort of football fan are you? (ir)

Green words: *Say the sounds. Say the word.*

whirl twirl first dirt girl firm thirst stir smirk

Say the syllables. Say the word.

stir → stirred play → playing → played

Red words:

what of are you to do your who they be*

Challenge words:

one world ball sounds draw most nose post try goal whistle ears

Vocabulary check: **fanatical** *a big fan* **smirk** *a small smile*

* These words are red for a while

Norman Knight, time-travelling superstar (ou)

Green words: *Say the sounds. Say the word.*

out pounce proud foul ground round sound doubt

Say the syllables. Say the word.

thou'sand → thousand as'tound → astound

Say the root word. Say the whole word.

bounce → bouncing astound → astounding

Red words:

to there are of what do you come won there go* he* we* no*

Challenge words:

down ball now only save take semi superstar goalie trying

Vocabulary check: **spuds** *potatoes* **stacks** *lots of*

Troy Tomato cooks up a storm (oy oi)

Green words: *Say the sounds. Say the word.*

Joy foil Troy oil boil boy joint spoil

Say the syllables. Say the word.

en'joy → enjoy sir'loin → sirloin

Say the root word. Say the whole word.

spoil → spoiled disappoint → disappointed

Red words:

would you to some of were what your all do are want was they call he* go* be* me* my* no* so*

Challenge words:

Tomato chef how auntie told always wash won't try pancakes like can't water chilli golden oven fire don't almost

Vocabulary check: **employ** *to give a job to somebody* **bangers** *sausages*

** These words are red for a while*